The Thinking TREE

www.DyslexiaGames.com

Dyslexia Games Series A Book 5
Friendly Copyright Notice:

The Thinking Tree LLC   ●   617 N Swope St.   ●   Greenfield, IN 46140   ●   info@dyslexiagames.com   ●   (317) 622-8852

Practice Pages

A Unique Method of Writing Symbols, Letters & Numbers. For Dyslexic Students.

By Sarah J. Brown

Parent Teacher Instructions:

Provide the student with a pencil, eraser, and a fine point black pen.

The student will practice copying the letter, number or symbol in each row.
You may wish to show the child how to form the symbol before he does it on his
own. The child will draw the symbol in each of the empty spaces (little books).

These practice pages will be very helpful to children who tend to reverse and confuse
certain letters and numbers.

Pages 20 –30 are blank so that you can write in the letters or numbers that the child
needs more time to practice.

Practice Pages

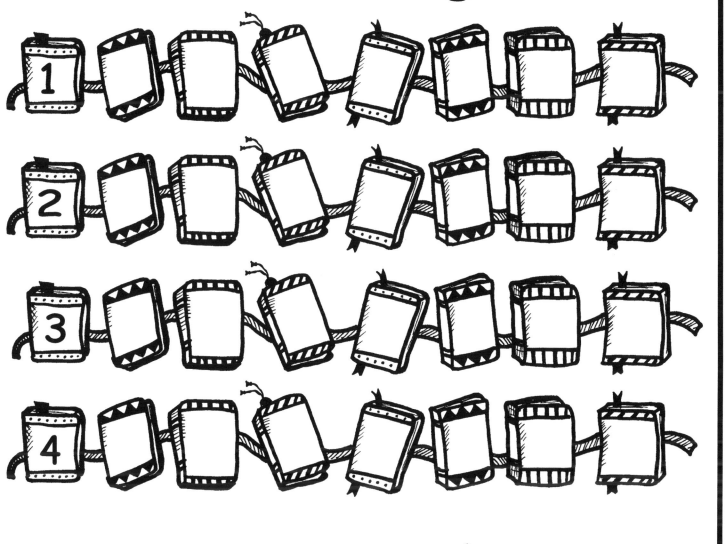

Name:_____ Date:_____

Practice Pages

Name:_____   **Date:**_____

Practice Pages

Name:_____ **Date:**_____

Practice Pages

Name:_____ **Date:**_____

Practice Pages

Name:_____ **Date:**_____

Practice Pages

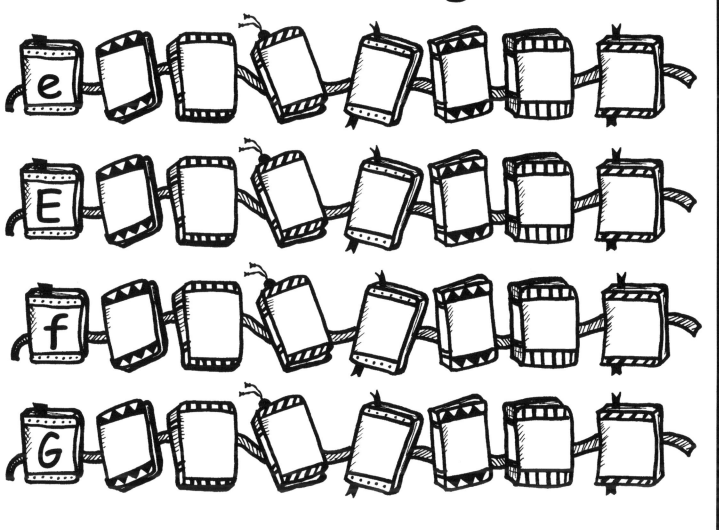

Name:_____   **Date:**_____

Practice Pages

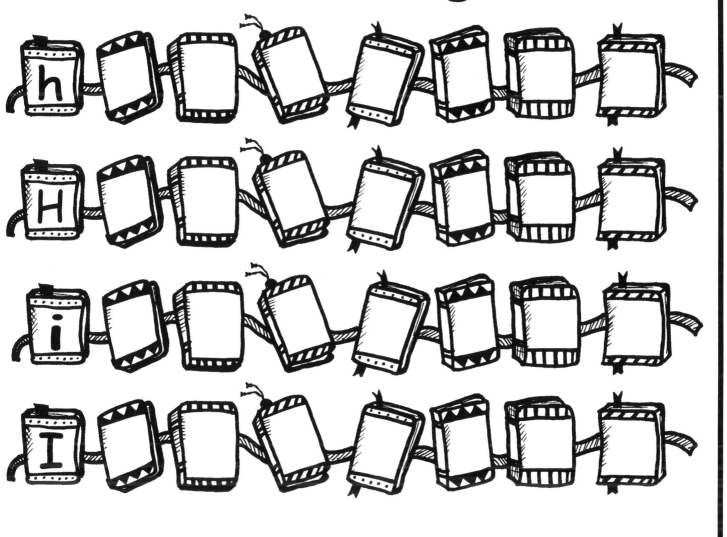

Practice Pages

Name:_____ **Date:**_____

Practice Pages

Name:_____ **Date:**_____

Practice Pages

Name:_____ **Date:**_____

Practice Pages

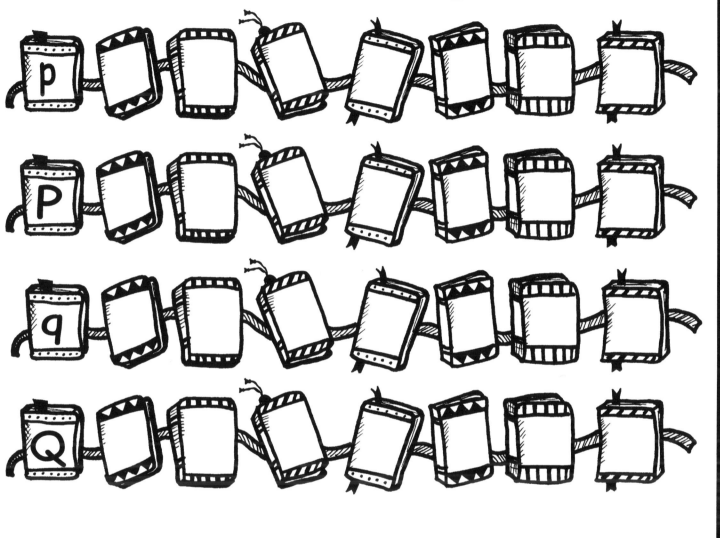

Name:_____   **Date:**_____

Practice Pages

r

R

s

S

Name:_____ Date:_____

Practice Pages

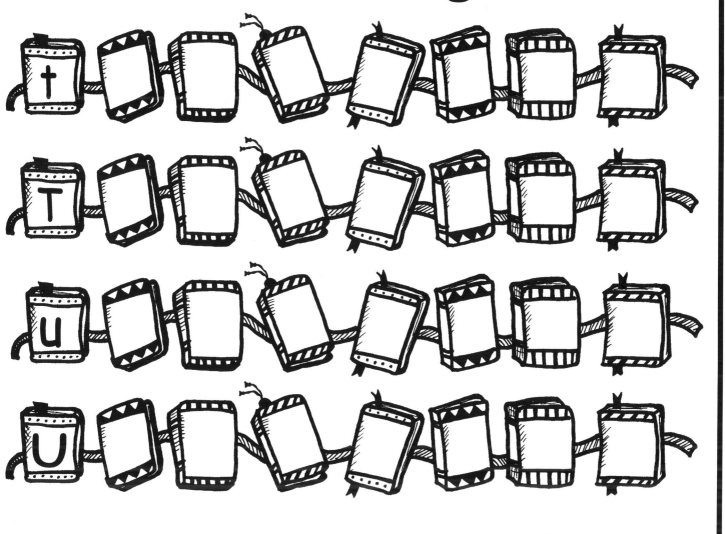

Name:_____ **Date:**_____

Practice Pages

Name:_____ Date:_____

Practice Pages

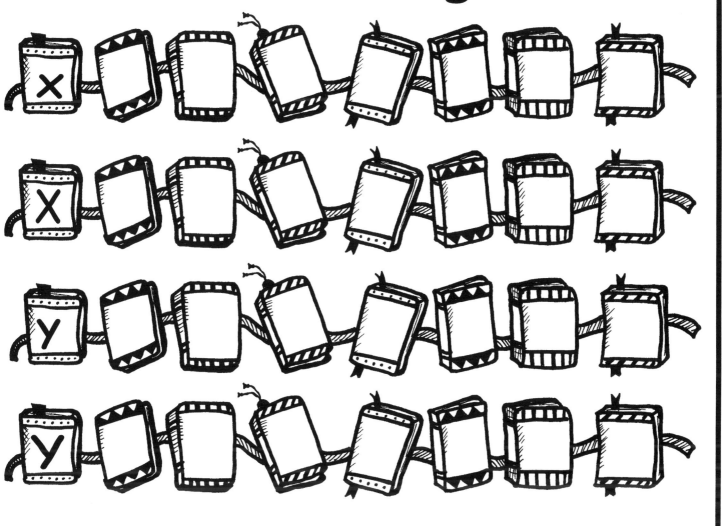

Name:_____ **Date:**_____

Practice Pages

Z

Z

?

!

Name:_____ Date:_____

Practice Pages

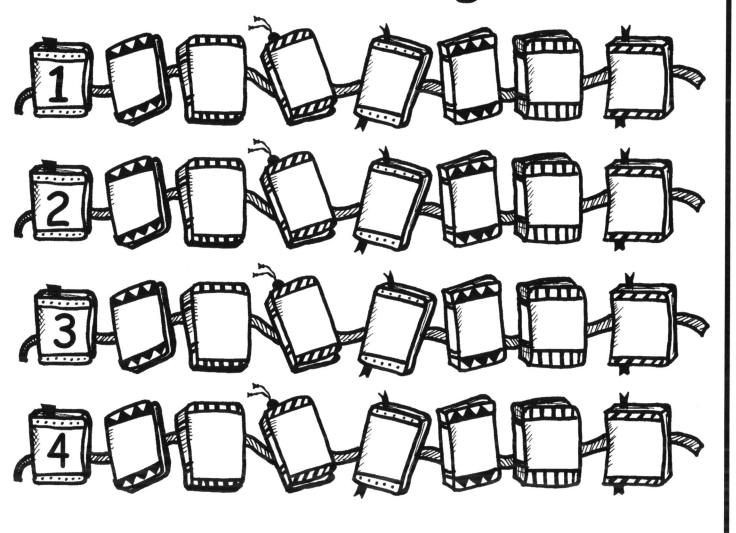

Name:_____ **Date:**_____

Practice Pages

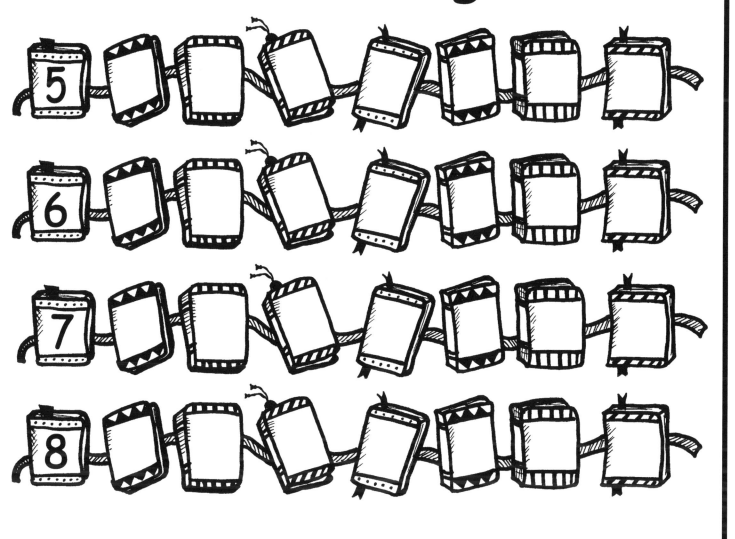

Name:_____ **Date:**_____

Practice Pages

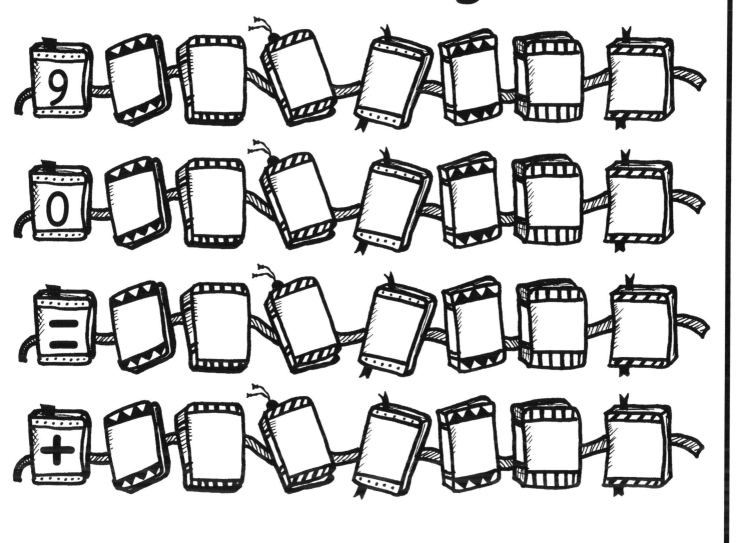

Name:_____ **Date:**_____

Make your own pattern

Name:_____ **Date:**_____

Practice Pages

Name:_____   **Date:**_____

Practice Pages

Name:_____ **Date:**_____

Practice Pages

Name:_____ Date:_____

Practice Pages

Name:_____ **Date:**_____

Practice Pages

Name:_____ **Date:**_____

Practice Pages

Practice Pages

Name:_____ **Date:**_____

Practice Pages

Name:_____ Date:_____

Practice Pages

Name:_____ Date:_____

Practice Pages

Name:_____ Date:_____

Practice Pages

Certificate of Completion

_____

Name & Age

_____

Date of Completion

The Thinking
TREE

_____

Teacher

The Thinking
TREE

www.DyslexiaGames.com

Created by: Sarah Janisse Brown

Made in the USA
Middletown, DE
21 August 2020